D1616187

DATE DUE

NC

THE PEN & INK AND CROSS HATCH STYLES OF

THE EARLY ILLUSTRATORS

THE PEN & INK AND CROSS HATCH STYLES OF
THE EARLY ILLUSTRATORS

A COPYRIGHT FREE HANDBOOK COMPILED BY DICK SUTPHEN

ART DIRECTION BOOK COMPANY

19 West 44th Street · New York, N.Y. 10036

CONTENTS

"The Early Illustrators" is a representative sampling of the finest pen and ink editorial illustrations from 1850 to 1920. I have included a balanced cross-section of styles, but the book is not intended to be an historic review of this period. Rather the material has been chosen for its reuse potential. This volume is the result of a ten year search — derived from hundreds of American and European sources. All of the illustrations are copyright-free, which means they may be used in advertising, publications, or on products — without additional permission or payment.

Dick Sutphen

1
Men

Moujik ivre —

7

Sebastian Cabot

Men

Men

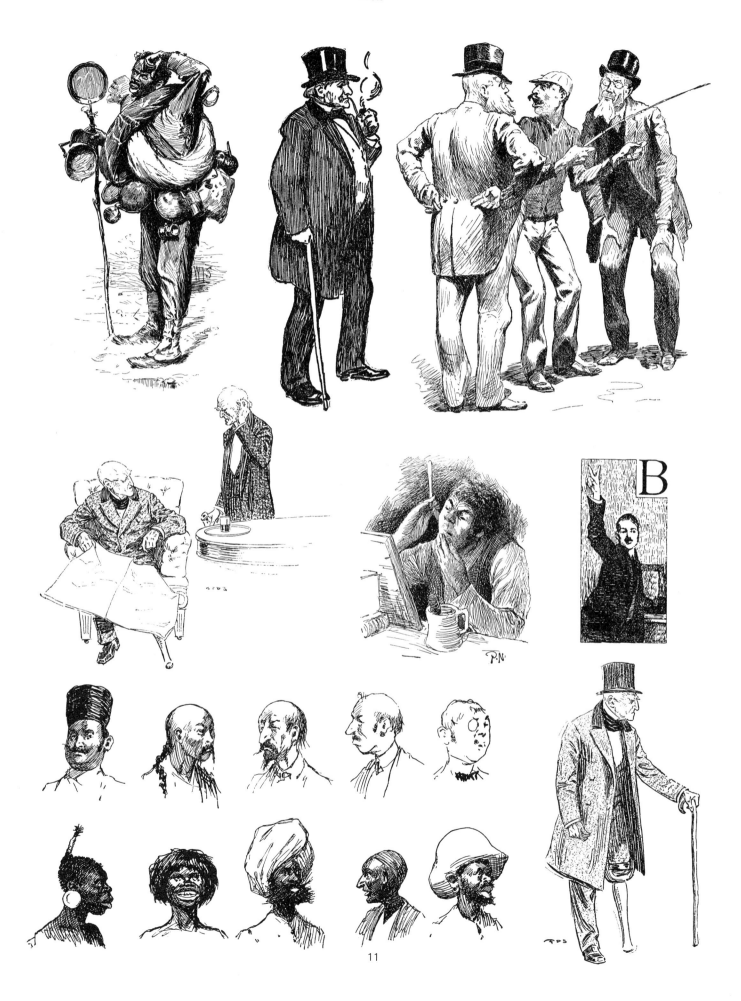

Men

15

Men

18

Men

2
Women

Frank Fowler.
1891.

WILD WOMAN OF THE CATSKILLS

3
Children
& CHILDREN'S BOOK ILLUSTRATIONS

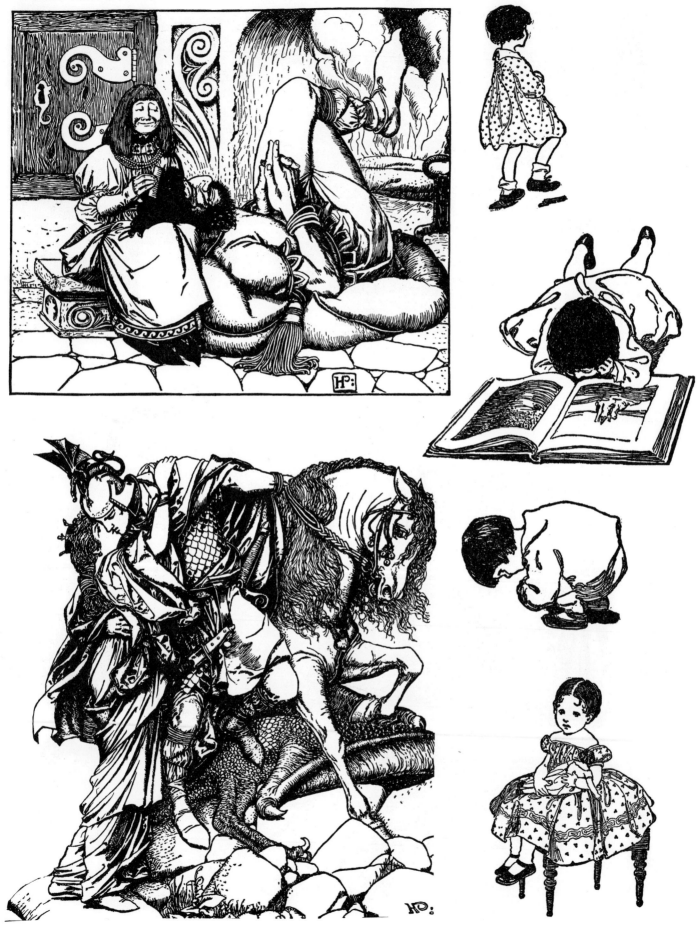

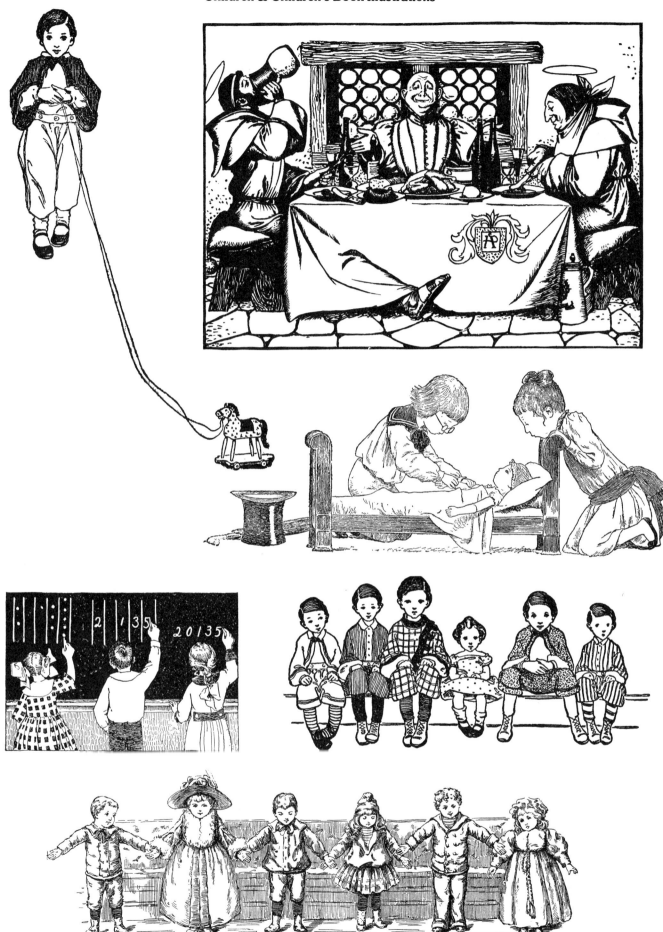

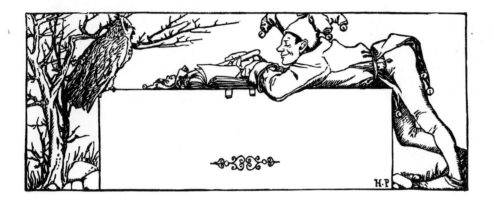

4
People
IN SITUATIONS

A DRIFT IN W. 1851

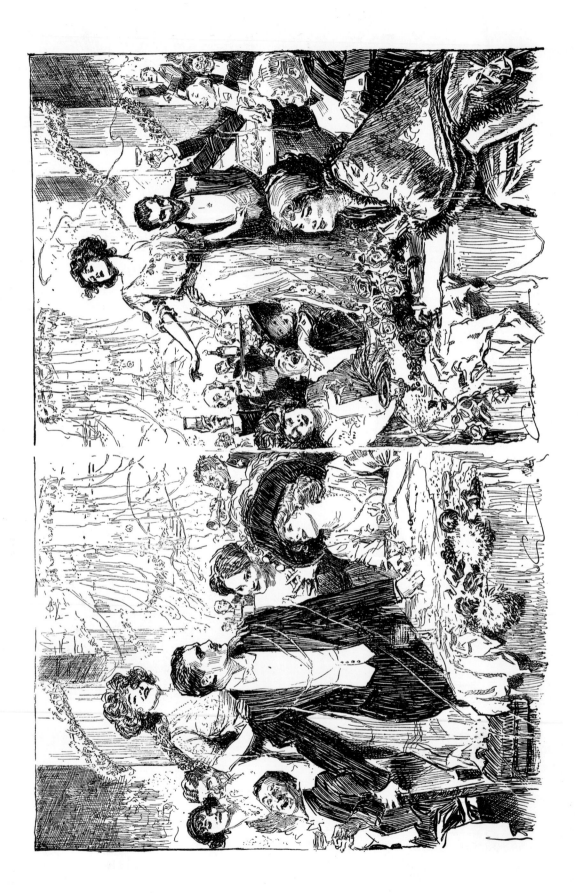

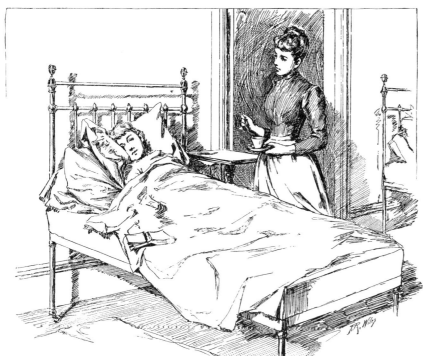

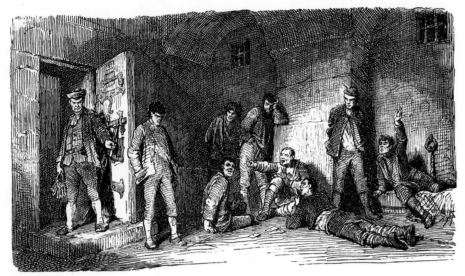

R.F Zogbaum

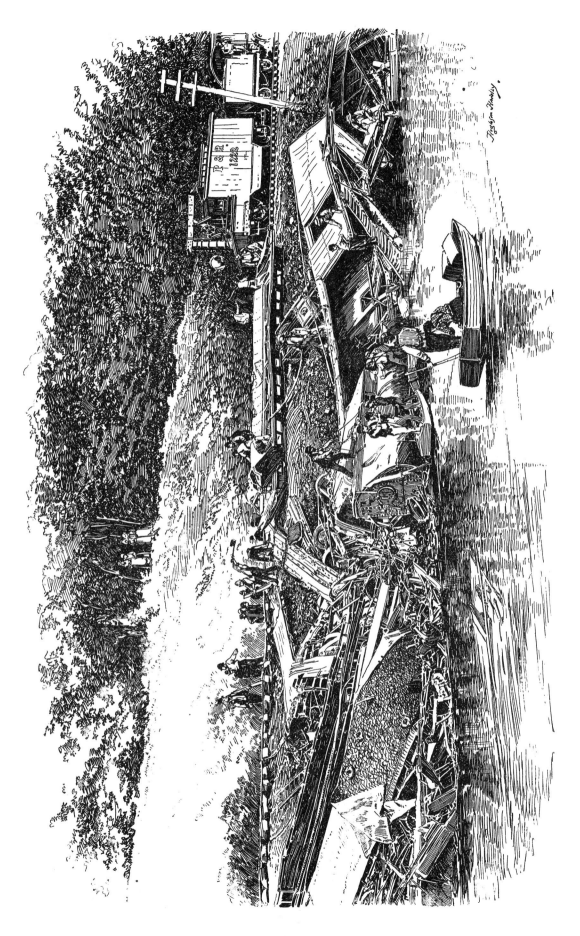

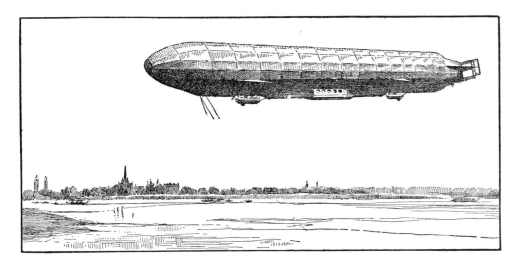

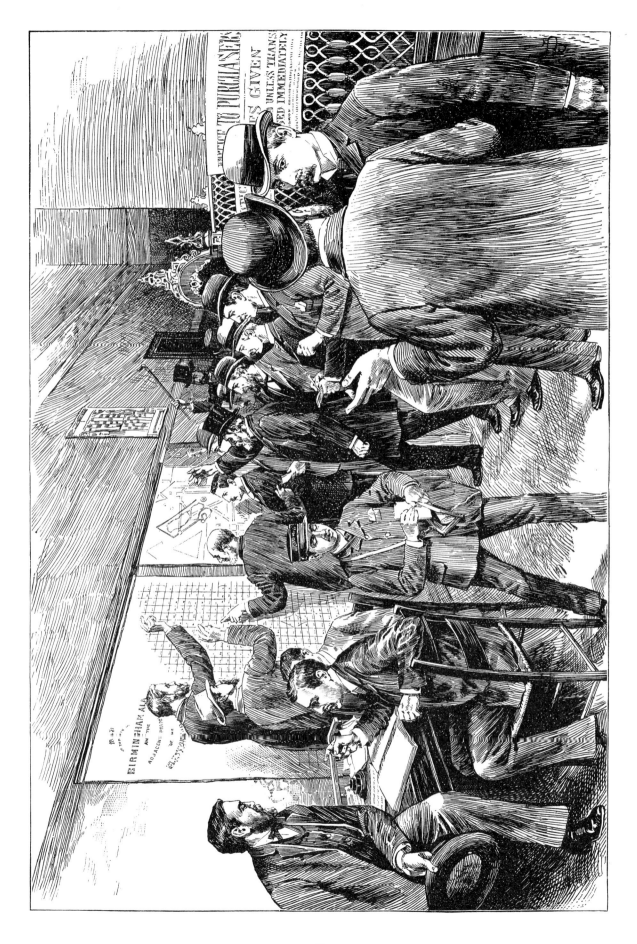

5
Western Scenes

San Carlos

"José Marie"

Packs

"The redertero horse"

"Dogged Washer"

Remington

Officer in Full Dress. — Mounted.

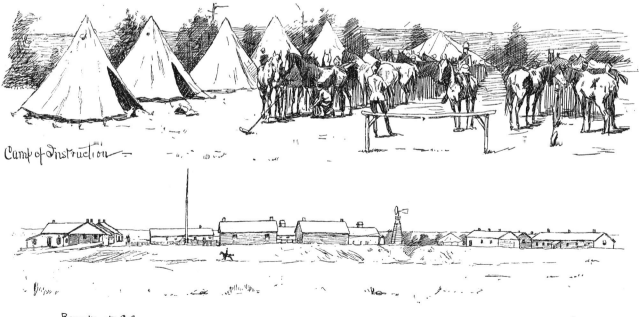

Camp of Instruction —

Barracks at Calgary —

Frederic Remington

6
❀ Period Dress ❀

Period Dress

106

·ALBERTVS ·II·

·FRIDERICVS·

ISABELLA

7
❦ The Cartoonists ❦

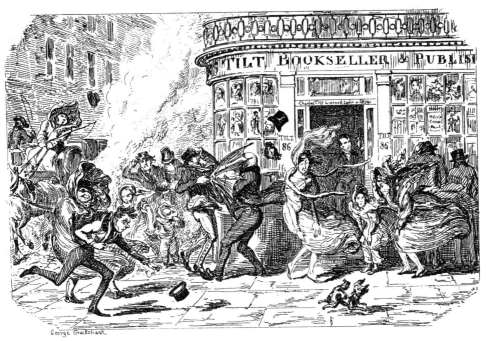

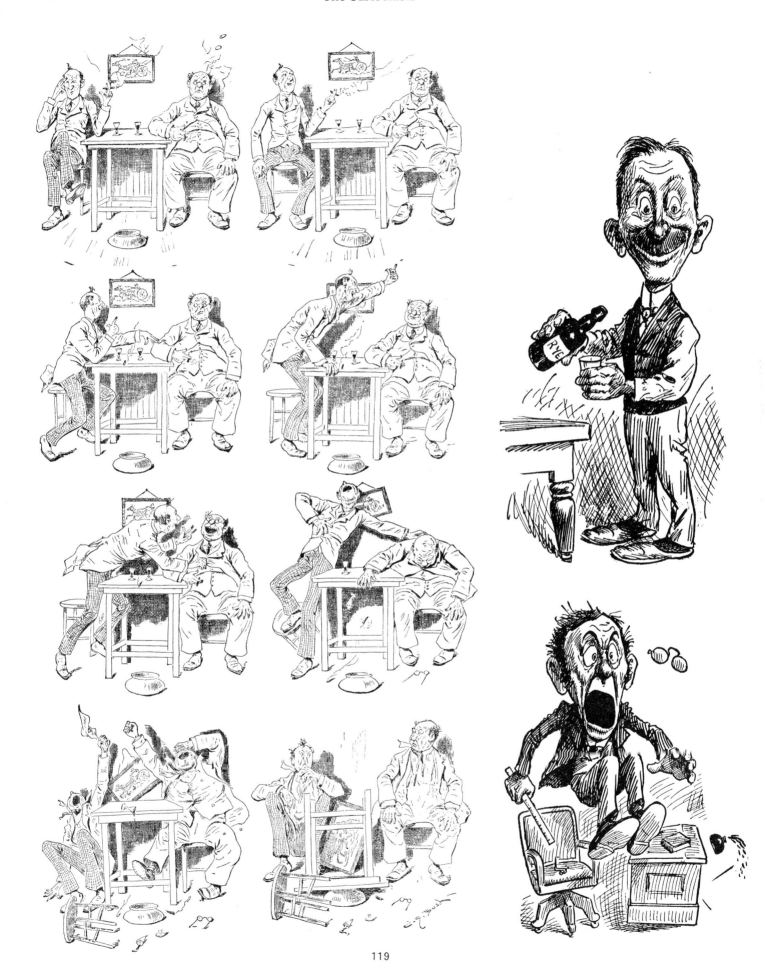

The Cartoonists

8
⊱ Rural ⊰

JULIEN-DUPRE. 1886

9
❧ Nautical ❧

10
⊱ Sports ⊰

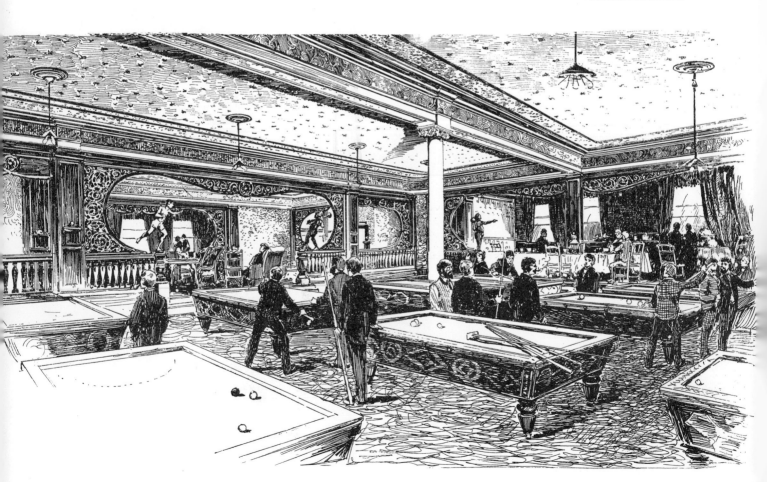

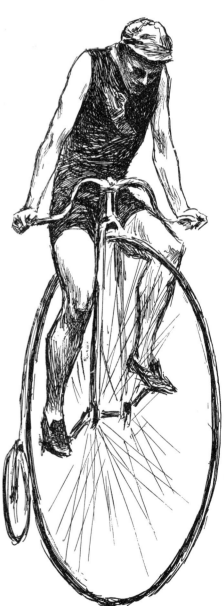

At the Races

The Skating Rink...

11
❧ Combat-Military ❧

12
The Environment

The Cathedral of Saint Machar

C.E.Flower

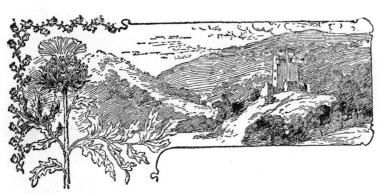

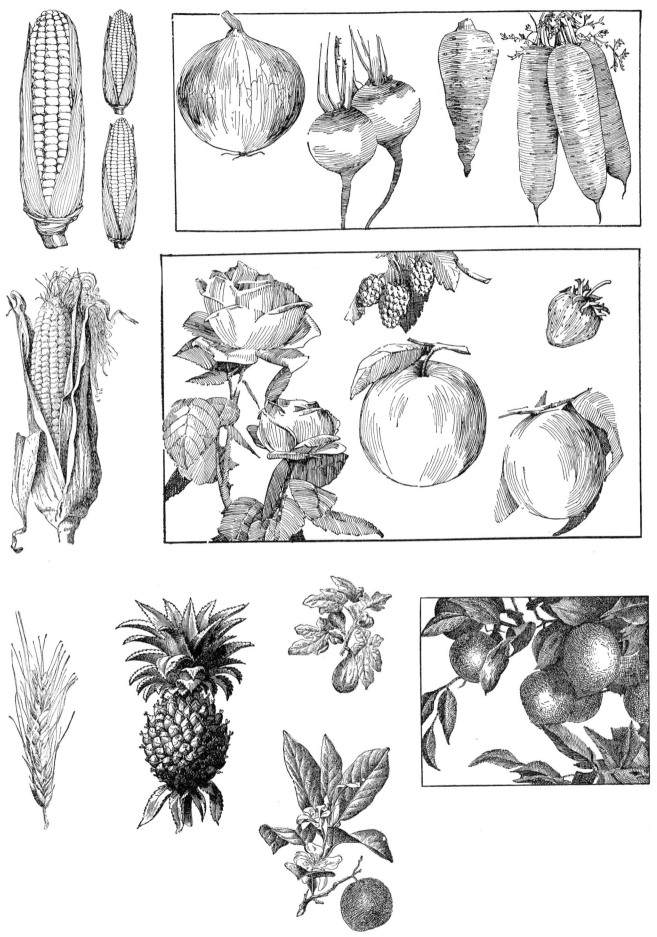

13
❧ Animals ❧

H·M·HAINES

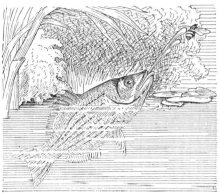

14
⊱ Architectural & City ⊰
ILLUSTRATIONS

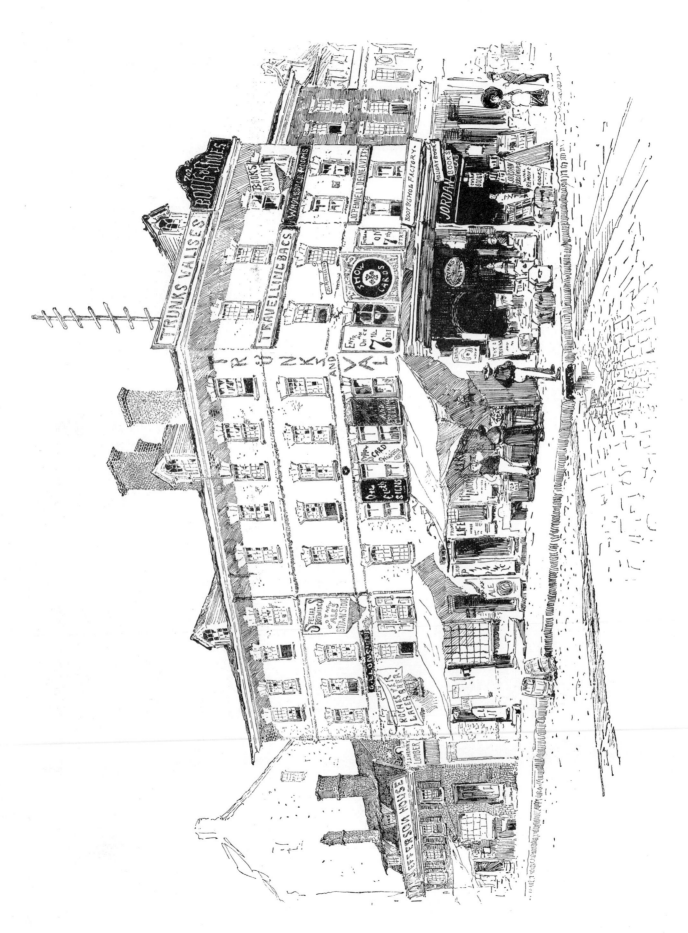

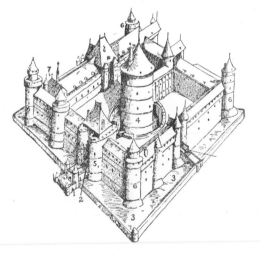

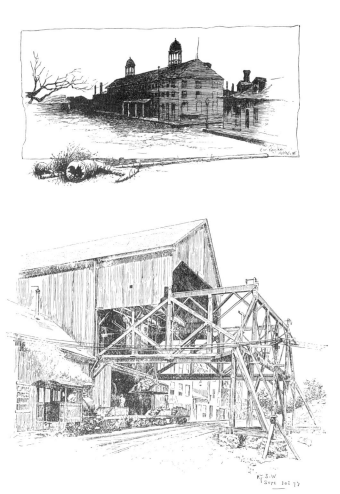

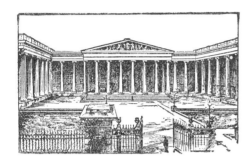

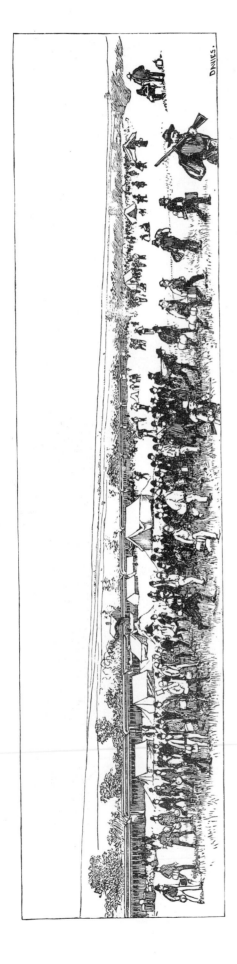

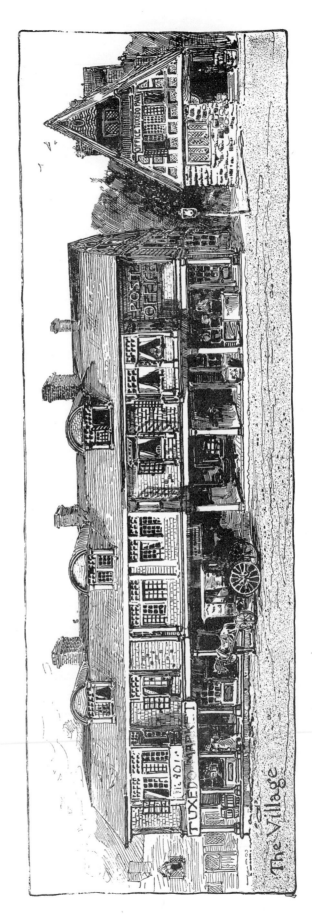

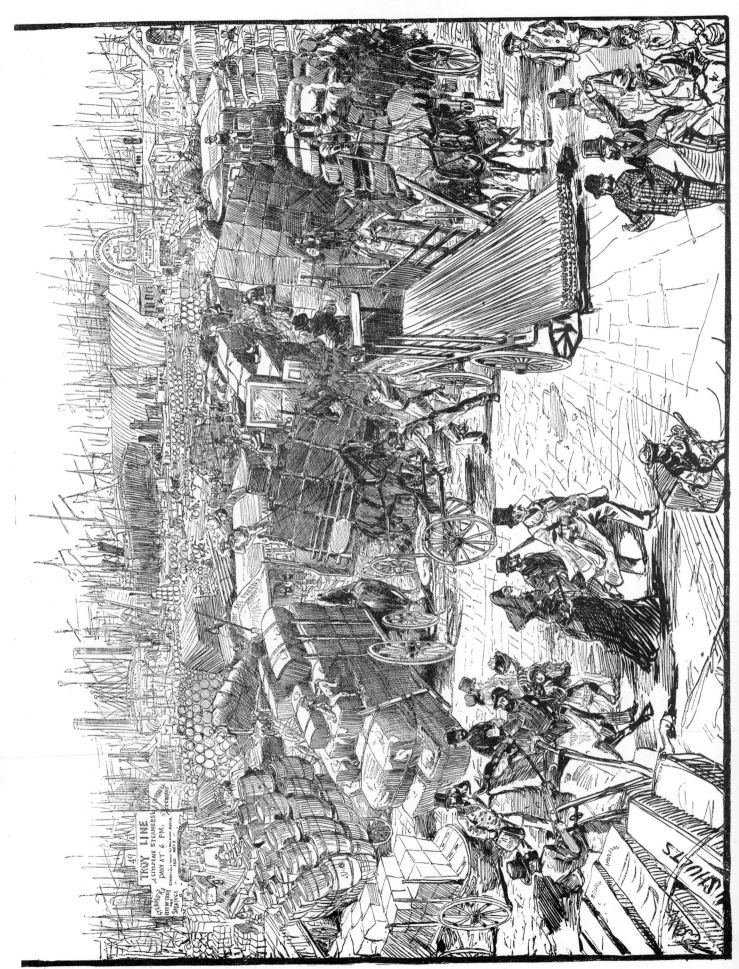

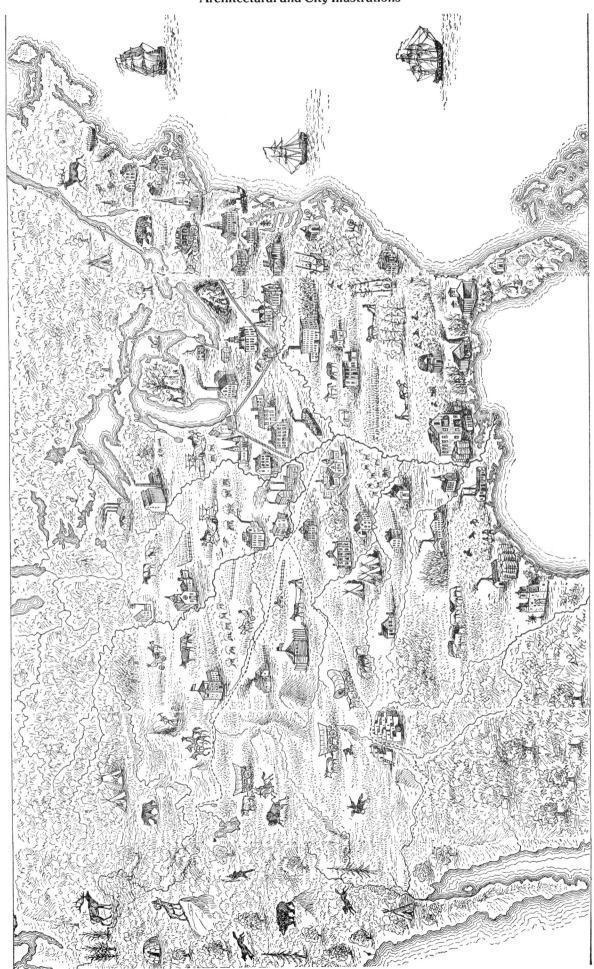

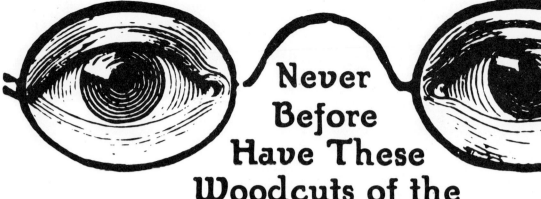

Never Before Have These Woodcuts of the 1880's Conner's Foundry Been Published in Facsimile For Your Immediate Use!

A MAGNIFICENT TREASURY OF OLD-TIME "SPOTS" FOR THE ART DIRECTOR, ARTIST AND DESIGNER

Everything You've Always Wanted in an **(1860's-1880's)** Swipe Library—But Were Afraid You'd Never Find

During the richly nostalgic 1860's, 1870's and 1880's, the vast variety of large and small "printer's electrotypes" sold by James Conner's Sons—also known as the United States Type Foundry—presented in minute detail the scenes, people, trades and pastimes of our growing nation.

These meticulously designed illustrations were godsends to the com-

4,419 Cuts FOR REFERENCE, STUDY AND REPRODUCTION

American Eagles	Sports and Pastimes
Flags and Stars	Houses and Mills
Zodiac Signs	Fish and Shellfish
Business Trade Cuts	Tobacco Products
Comic Displays	Beverages
Hands and Fists	Musical Instruments
Birds and Animals	Printing Presses
Race Horses, Cattle	Fraternal Emblems
Ships and Boats	Religious Pictures
Steam Locomotives	State Seals, Crests
Fire Engines	Coins and Medals
Hats and Shoes	Masqueraders
China and Glassware	Allegorical Views
Clocks and Watches	Panels, Cartouches
Trade Tools	Decorative Initials
House Furnishings	*and much more*

munications media of their time. Nothing quite like them had ever been offered before, and nothing quite the same has been created since.

For the small-town newspaper, the handbill advertiser, the job printer far removed from big-city artwork and engravers, these ready-to-use pictures were virtually the only means of brightening the printed page.

For the business announcement or auction sale, these cuts provided visual interest for the reader that was unattainable with type alone. As illustrators of merchandise, they were the life-blood of the then emerging mail-order catalog . . . and in quickening the American economy, they contributed to the development of the whole world of advertising.

Today these century-old "stock electros" reflect with incomparable fidelity the design, the taste, the tempo of American life in the second half of the 19th Century. They are a matchless source of ideas for layout, campaign themes, old-time atmosphere, attention-commanding spots.

Any of the 4,419 specimens in this great collection may now be reproduced in any manner desired. The special Introduction by Paul Duensing is a concise history of this germinal era in American illustration. At $19.50 postpaid, this large volume—200 thronged pages, 10¼ x 13½" in size, clearly printed on fine smooth paper and durably bound—is a superb "buy."

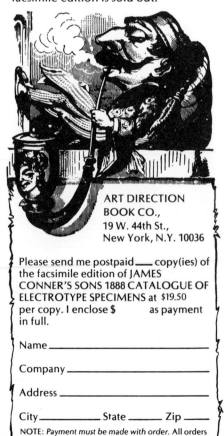